Energy And Action

ENERGY AT WORK

John Marshall, Ed.D.

The Rourke Book Co., Inc.
Vero Beach, Florida 32964

© 1995 The Rourke Book Co., Inc.

PHOTO CREDITS
All photos © J.M. Patten

Library of Congress Cataloging-in-Publication Data

Marshall, John, 1944-
    Energy at work / by John Marshall.
        p. cm. — (Energy and action)
    Includes index.
    Summary: Explains the relationship between energy and work, as
defined scientifically.
    ISBN 1-55916-153-1
    1. Force and energy—Juvenile literature. [1. Force and energy.
2. Work (Mechanics)] I. Title. II. Series.
QC73.M37 1995
531'.6—dc20
                                    95-13499
                                            CIP
                                            AC

Printed in the USA

TABLE OF CONTENTS

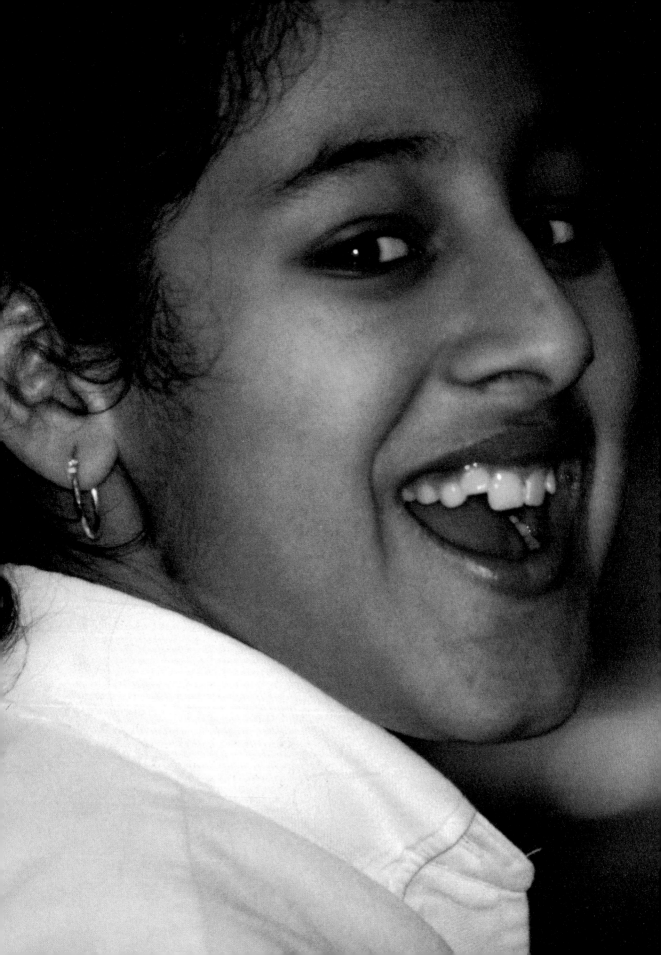

WORK IN OUR WORLD

What does **work** (WERK) mean to you? Does it mean doing homework, or maybe cleaning the garage?

An artist may think of a favorite painting as a work of art. A dentist works on teeth. Your teacher may ask you to work out a math problem.

Let's read all about what the word work means in science. You may be surprised at first, but that's what makes science fun. You never know what you will find out!

Children make good scientists because they like to think, wonder and ask, "Why?"

WORK IN THE SCIENTIST'S WORLD

The scientist in you is going to think about work in a new and different way.

Work is when a **force** (FORS) moves an object. A force is simply a push or a pull. If you fly a kite—that's work. The force of the wind moves the kite around the sky.

This man's job is to protect the community from fire and to help other people.

The worker is pushing a large roll of plastic used to cover a swimming pool.

It takes a big force to move a school bus down the street. An entire class of children can push or pull with all their might and not be able to move it one inch.

The tired students may feel they did a lot of work by pushing and pulling hard. However, because the bus didn't move, scientists would say no work was done at all.

HOW MUCH WORK?

Work comes in all sizes. We can do a little work or a lot of work.

To learn how scientists look at work, pretend you are pulling your little brother in his wagon. You are using force to move the wagon along.

Now think about what will happen if your little sister climbs in, too. You will have to pull harder, or use a bigger force, to move the heavier load.

You did more work because you used more force.

It takes less work to move an empty bus than a bus full of students.

BIG DISTANCE—BIG WORK

It's funny to think that every time you enjoy a bike ride you are actually doing work. Your feet push down on the pedals, moving the bicycle forward.

You may ride your bike around the block or around the world. The farther you go, the more work you do.

Distance (DIS tens) is the space between two places. Scientists tell us that the farther you move something, the more work you've done.

These kids don't have a big enough force to do the work of moving this wall.

WHERE DOES FORCE COME FROM?

Force and distance are important words to know when you talk about work. Let's find out where force actually comes from. What is it that makes all the pushes and pulls of force possible?

Energy (EN er jee) is the special power that makes force. People and machines use energy to do work.

Leg muscles are the force that move bicycles.

This machine has enough force to push a lot of dirt a long distance.

Some kinds of energy move, like wind or running water. Wind blowing leaves across the lawn is a form of what scientists call **kinetic energy** (ki NET ik EN er jee)—the energy of motion.

Energy that does not move is called **potential energy** (poh TEN shul EN er jee). Potential energy is stored until it is used. Your muscles have potential energy when you are asleep.

ENERGY FROM DIFFERENT PLACES

People get energy from healthy foods. Your body digests, or breaks down, a hamburger or a plate of spaghetti into energy. Food becomes the power that allows your muscles to push and pull.

We can't feed peanut butter and jelly sandwiches to snow blowers and tractors for energy. Machines use a fuel like gasoline. Gasoline burns in an engine, giving off the energy it uses to work.

Some machines get their energy from electricity. Others get it from wind or water. No matter what the source, it always takes energy to do work.

People get the energy to work from eating food.

ENERGY STARTS WITH THE SUN

The story of energy and where it comes from starts at a place very far away. In fact, it's not even on Earth. It's the sun!

The sun has a very big supply of energy. It gives its energy through sunlight to the plants. Plants grow and pass that energy along to animals and people who eat them.

Eating a juicy peach is a great way to give our bodies energy. The peach tree uses the sun's energy to grow and make the peach. The sun gives some of its energy to the peach tree, and then the peach tree passes the energy on to us in the peach that we eat.

All of the Earth's energy comes from the sun.

ENERGY HIDES DEEP IN THE EARTH

It is easy to see that energy from food really comes from the sun. Where does the energy in gasoline come from?

Gasoline is made from oil. Oil forms underground over millions of years from dead plants and animals. Without the sun, these old plants and animals would never have lived.

The sun helped make the gasoline that will give this car its energy.

The electricity you turn on is energy made from oil with the sun's help.

Today, oil is pumped from deep inside the Earth and turned into gasoline. Burning gasoline makes the energy that runs many machines.

Oil also helps make energy. Special buildings called power stations burn the oil to run machines called **generators** (JEN er ay terz). Generators make the electricity that we use to turn on lights, play video games and run computers.

That far-away star we call our sun is the source of all our energy.

THE WORLD IS FULL OF WORK

Work can mean many different things to people. It may be cleaning your room, studying for a test or trying to wash your cat.

The scientist part of you, however, knows that work is only done when a force moves an object. The amount of work that is done depends on how big the force is and how far the object is moved.

Energy is the power that makes work happen. Without the sun, there would be no energy. Without energy, the world would be still and quiet, and no work could ever be done.

Firemen go to "work." Fire trucks work every time they race to a fire.

GLOSSARY

distance (DIS tens) — the space between two places

energy (EN er jee) — the power behind force

force (FORS) — the push and pull that makes things move

generator (JEN er ay ter) — a machine that produces electricity

kinetic energy (ki NET ik EN er jee) — moving energy

potential energy (poh TEN shul EN er jee) — stored energy

work (WERK) — a force moving an object over a distance

This girl has energy to ride her bike. She eats healthy food every day.

INDEX